Copyr

CW00432798

Table of Contents

1 Oktoberfest Background

The first Oktoberfest was held on 17 October 1810 in honor of the wedding of Prince Ludwig of Bavaria with Princess Therese of Sachsen-Hildburghausen.

Back then it was just a horse race and not yet the big event it is today. Apparently, though, the horse race was such a success, the people wanted to repeat it. So, the Oktoberfest was born and has since been celebrated year after year with just a few exceptions during war and times of cholera and plague.

Over time, the festival became more and more popular and slowly changed into the event we know now: food stalls and fun rides were added, the famous *Hendl* (chicken) was sold, the horse race was abandoned in favor of the beer tents, etc.

As the Oktoberfest grew longer, from one day in the beginning to the 16 to 18 days now, the opening date was changed to begin in September. This is due to the weather in Germany. At the end of October weather can be rather unpleasant and cold; in some years it even starts snowing. Therefore, it would be much too cold to sit outside in the beer gardens or enjoy the rides.

Unfortunately, the Oktoberfest also has its dark points: In 1980 the assassin Gundolf Köhler detonated a bomb near the main entrance, 13 people were killed and more than 200 injured. In memory of these victims, there's a memorial at the main entrance.

Today, the Oktoberfest in Munich is the biggest folk festival in the world with more than 6 million visitors. It has become more and more a beer festival with emphasis on the beer tents with music and dancing on the benches.

But it keeps on changing and in 2010 the *Oide Wiesn* (old-fashioned Oktoberfest) was introduced. This is held every other year in the southern part of Theresienwiese and relives the old times with old fashioned merry-go-rounds, beer tents without party music, but more traditional Bavarian music, etc.

This is the place to go for families with kids. Everything is much quieter and less crowded.

2 The Festival

I took the picture below from the Ferris wheel and it shows the part of Oktoberfest grounds where all the fun rides are

When the Oktoberfest was first held, the location was still a meadow. You remember they conducted a horse race in honor of the royal bridal couple, right? The German word for meadow is "Wiese" and in honor of Princess Therese it was from then on called "Theresienwiese".

This is the reason why we locals affectionately call the Oktoberfest *Wiesn*, as a short form of Theresienwiese. Say *Wiesn* instead of Oktoberfest, and you're one of us.

2.1 Location Map

On the map below you can see the Oktoberfest grounds
with the nearest Underground stations as well as the
location of all the big tents. The part on the right side,
along the "Schaustellerstraße" is reserved for the fun
rides.

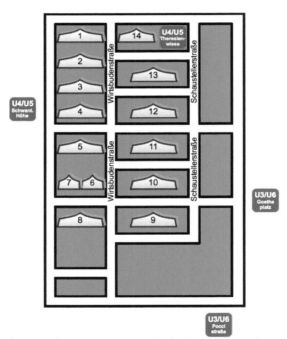

1 = Hippodrom   2 = Armbrustschützenzelt
3 = Hofbräuzelt   4 = Hackerzelt
5 = Schottenhamel   6 = Winzerer Fähndl
7 = Schützenfesthalle   8 = Käfer's Wiesnschänke
9 = Weinzelt   10 = Löwenbräuzelt
11 = Bräurosl   12 = Augustiner Festzelt
13 = Ochsenbraterei   14 = Fischer-Vroni

2.2 Opening Hours and Important Events

The famous opening ceremony, the *Anstich* dates back to 1950. This was the first time when the then mayor of Munich Thomas Wimmer, opened the first barrel of beer in the Schottenhamel tent while everyone watched. From then on the Anstich has become an important ceremony on the opening day and our current mayor Christian Ude has perfected his technique of opening the wooden barrel with a hammer up to the point where he needs only two to three whacks.

With the famous words **Ozapft Is**, he officially opens the Oktoberfest and has the privilege to give the first Mass beer to the Bavarian prime minister.

Anstich takes place exactly at noon, right after the opening parade. It's traditional that nobody is served beer before then. Even though people flock to the tents as early as 6 a.m. in order to secure a great place, only soft drinks are sold until the Oktoberfest is officially opened a few minutes after noon.

Even then, you can't count on a speedy delivery of your first Oktoberfest beer, because all the other 10.000 visitors in your tent want one too, so it can take a while until the waitress can deliver the backlog of orders.

Official Opening Hours

2013	21 September, noon until 6 October 11:30 p.m.
2014	20 September, noon until 5 October 11:30 p.m
2015	19 September, noon until 4 October 11:30 p.m

Beer Tents

Weekdays: 10 a.m. Until 11:30 p.m. (Käfers Wiesnschänke and Weinzelt until 1 a.m.)

Weekend and 3 October: 9 a.m. Until 11:30 p.m. (Käfers Wiesnschänke and Weinzelt until 1 a.m.)

Last orders: 10:30p.m.

Fun Rides

Weekdays: 10 a.m. Until 11:30 p.m.

Friday and Saturday: 10 a.m. until midnight

Family Day (with discounts)

Tuesday: noon until 6 p.m.

Mittagswiesn (Lunch discounts)

Weekdays 10 a.m. until 3 p.m.

Opening Parade

21 September 2013   11 a.m.

Trachten und Schützenumzug (traditional costume parade)

22 September 2013   10 a.m.

Traditional concert of the Oktoberfest brass bands at the feet of the Bavaria monument

29 September 2013   11 a.m.

Traditional gun salute on the steps of the Bavaria monument.

6 October 2013   noon

2.3 Wiesn Rules

Oh yes, we Germans have rules for everything, including the Oktoberfest! Below are the official rules from the city of Munich (translated by me).

No access to the site between 1:30 a.m. and 6 a.m.

No weapons, including knifes, sticks, glass bottles, etc.

No inline skates, skateboards, etc. Bikes have to be left at the entrance.

No peeing outside the toilets.

No pets except seeing-eye dogs for the blind.

No kids under 16 after 8 p.m. (except accompanied by their parents). Kids under 6 must always be with their parents and aren't allowed in the beer tents after 8 p.m.

Strollers and prams (baby carriages) are allowed until 6.p.m. except on Saturdays when they are not allowed at all.

No painting, graffiti or vandalism.

You're not allowed to bring you own alcoholic beverages.

No selling of goods except with proper authorization from the City of Munich.

Everyone who doesn't adhere to the rules can be expelled from Oktoberfest grounds.

2.4 Baggage Deposit

It's not a good idea to bring big backpacks, or other luggage to the Oktoberfest. You might lose them some tents don't allow them in, especially later in the evening.

If you can't leave your stuff in your accommodation, there's a baggage deposit located directly at the entrance to the Underground station **Theresienwiese**. When you exit the underground station, turn to your right, and there it is.

The price is 2,70 Euro per piece per day and the opening hours are 11 a.m. To 11 p.m. on weekdays and 11 a.m. to midnight on Friday and Saturday nights.

If you plan to stay up partying the whole night, the closing time for the luggage deposit is much too early for you. Furthermore there will probably be a long queue when you arrive or leave with everyone else.

Therefore, I recommend the baggage lockers at Hauptbahnhof (central station). They're open 24 hours a day. Prices are similar, they could even work out cheaper if you take one of the very big lockers and share with your friends.

Just make sure you don't lose the key! Write down the number of the luggage locker somewhere. If you happen to lose the key, you can still go to the locker administrators and ask them to open the locker. You will of course need to know the locker number, have your passport handy and give a good description of what is inside (It would be good to have a piece of paper with your name inside the locker, this will be proof that the suitcases are really yours.) But you won't lose the key, right?

2.5 Lost and Found

Believe it or not, thousands of items are lost every year during the festival and turned in to the authorities. The Oktoberfest has its very own lost and found (Fundbüro). It's located behind the Schottenhamel beer tent.

Opening hours are from from 12:30 p.m. To 11 p.m. daily (Phone: 089 23 33 02 98).

After the festival the items are transferred to the Munich lost and found office and are kept for six months before they're auctioned off.

3 How to Get There

Public transport will be crowded, but it's still the best way to get to the Oktoberfest grounds. The Munich Transport Company (MVG) does its best to bring everyone safely to Theresienwiese.

The underground lines U4 and U5 stop directly at **Theresienwiese** and offer the shortest walk to the tents. During the Wiesn these lines will run every two to fife minutes. Still, they're always packed and smell like beer. But don't worry, it's only a very short ride.

Have a look at the picture below to get the impression.

Another possibility is to take the lines U3 and U6 to **Goetheplatz**. They're less crowded, but it's a slightly longer walk (approx. 10 minutes) to the Wiesn.

Depending on where you stay, the S-Bahn is also an option. From the station **Hackerbrücke** it's a 10 minute walk with thousands of other visitors to the

Theresienwiese. All S-Bahn lines stop at Hackerbrücke and they run every one to two minutes in the city center.

Taxis are also an option, but can become quite difficult. During rush hour you might have to wait a long time. This is the best season for the taxis and they're all booked. The taxi companies even contract taxi drivers from other cities to give faster service to all the waiting clients.

If you stay in the center of Munich near Hauptbahnhof you can also walk, which might even be faster.

4 The Parades

On the first weekend of Oktoberfest you can watch two parades, which are both fascinating. On the map at http://www.inside-munich.com/octoberfest-breweries.html the itinerary of the opening parade on Saturday is marked in blue; the route of the costume parade (Trachten- und Schützenumzug) on Sunday is in red.

In order to get a good view and stand in the first line you should arrive at least half an hour before the start. If you're willing to spend 24,50 Euro you can buy tickets for one of these three outlets:

Sonnenstrasse in front of the bank "Hausbank"

Sonnenstrasse in front of Lindberg

Sonnenstrasse where the little lawn is

You can buy tickets at Muenchen Ticket. (but you must do it months in advance).

4.1 Opening Parade (Einzug der Wirte)

The opening parade is always on the first Saturday and starts at 10:50 a.m. It starts on *Sonnenstrasse*, follows *Schwanthalerstrasse* until it reaches the Theresienwiese. In total a 5 km long course is closed to traffic. During one hour all the owners of the big beer tents proceed in their horse-drawn carriages to the Theresienwiese. This, of course, is a relic from the past when the breweries actually used these carriages to transport the beer.

A good place to stand is Schwanthalerstrasse near the corner to Schillerstrasse.

I recommend watching the festive opening procession and head afterwards to the Theresienwiese. Usually, you can still get into one of the tents with exception of the Schottenhamel tent, where the *Anstich* takes place. You don't have to hurry, it might even be better to arrive there after 1 p.m., when everyone already has their first beer, and the waitresses are more relaxed and faster.

The most famous beer brewery is undoubtedly Hofbräu. You've probably heard about the Hofbräuhaus in Munich. Here is their carriage:

The carriages are brightly decorated and carry the most important ingredient of the Oktoberfest: the beer in wooden barrels. Most of the breweries use steel barrels now and carry the wooden ones only for decoration.

4.2 Traditional Costume Parade

We have many clubs that are dedicated to keeping the old traditions alive. The *Trachtenvereine* and the shooting clubs are invited to march with their traditional costumes in the Trachten- und Schützenumzug.

You will be amazed by the variety of different traditional clothing. Almost 10.000 people from hundreds of different groups form this parade, that not only shows you the widest variety of German and Bavarian traditional clothing but also features folk dance bands with drums, trumpets and marching songs.

The traditional costume parade takes place on the first Oktoberfest Sunday at 10 a.m. and lasts about two hours. If this seems too long for you, you can always chose to skip the rest of the parade and head straight for a refreshing mass of beer.

The route is about twice as long as the opening parade, and there is plenty of space where you can get a good look.

5 Enjoy the Fun Rides

There are many carnival rides at Oktoberfest in Munich. Apart from the nostalgic, old-fashioned ones you won't see anywhere else, we always have the latest and most exiting rides too. If you're daring, you'll love the adrenalin rush they'll give you.

They all have different prices, and as a rule of thumb you can say the more exciting it is, the higher the price. Most of them are probably in the range of four to eight Euro per person. Tuesday until 6 p.m. is family day when most of the rides have discounted prices.

Below are a few examples of what to expect, but you really have to walk through the Oktoberfest grounds to see what interests you most.

Toboggan Ride

The toboggan has appeared at the Oktoberfest in Munich for 70 years and is still as funny as ever. This is one of the rides where the spectators have a lot more fun watching than the participants trying to keep their balance. We never miss it!

Roller Coaster

The Oktoberfest always features several roller coasters. Ranging from the kid's coaster called *Wilde Maus* (wild mouse) to the Olympic looping one you can see in the picture above.

Teufelsrad (Devil's Wheel)

Consider an arena with a turning wheel in the center. You feel like a gladiator? Try to keep yourself from falling while the moderator makes fun of you. And all the other visitors are watching. It is a big laugh for everyone, spectators as well as the ones on the wheel. You can enter any time and stay as long as you want.

Free Fall

It's 50 meters high in the air and then the machine just drops you! This is definitely the one ride I'll never do again.

6 Guide to the Beer Tents

The beer tents are the heart of Oktoberfest and you can choose from 14 big tents with six different beer brands from Munich's breweries. We've been to all of them, some we like more than others. I'm sure you'll find your own favorite beer tent!

Personally, I think the perfect day at the Wiesn is to go first and ride a few of the fun rides, eat roasted almonds and then head for one of the beer tents. Stay a few hours, drink some beer or radler and leave before everyone else gets too drunk. :-)
By the way, the tents are not really tents anymore. Nowadays, they are made of steel and wood almost like houses. Because of the many visitors (a few thousands per tent) it would be much too dangerous otherwise.

Many guide books recommend that you move around from one tent to the next to get more variety. In theory this is good advice, but only as long as the tents are open. I don't recommend leaving your tent after 4 p.m., because you might not be let in anywhere else.

6.1 Hippodrom

The first beer tent at the entrance to Theresienwiese is easily recognized by the yellow and red color. It's one of the smaller tents, about half the size of the biggest ones. What makes this tent different is the Champagne bar where lots of in-people and celebrities hang out.

The music is great and I really like the decorations. But beware, it's a celebrity's beer tent and it's almost impossible to get inside in the evening or on the weekends. Try during the week around lunch time, and you're up for a great time!

There are two bands. During afternoon the more traditional one „Simmisamma" and in the evening the „Münchner Zwietracht". They also have a balcony for smokers.

Beer served: Spaten-Franziskaner.

www.hippodrom-oktoberfest.de

6.2 Armbrustschützenzelt

This is one of the biggest tents, with around 7500 seats. The name Armbrust means crossbow. You can already imagine that in the audience are many members of shooting clubs. The tent has its own shooting area but „nonshooters usually don't get to see that part.)

The music is provided by the band „Platzl". Smokers have a separate area in the garden near the main entrance. It's one of the favorite beer tents of some of my female friends because of the cute archers you can meet there :-)

Beer served: Paulaner.

www.armbrustschuetzenzelt.de

6.3 Hofbräuzelt

You probably have heard about the famous Hofbräuhaus.
This picture is the beer tent at the Oktoberfest. It might
be the most popular tent among the tourists. Here you're
guaranteed to meet many fellow travelers, especially
Americans and Australians.

The bands „Plattlinger Isarspatzen" and „Münchner
Gschichten" have adapted their music repertoire to the
international audience, which means once in a while you
hear an English song.

Beer served: Hofbräu

www.hb-festzelt.de

6.4 Hackerzelt

One of the biggest beer tents with almost 10 000 seats, the tent caters to people from the countryside around Munich. If you want to see authentic traditional clothing, your best chances are here. The music is more traditional.

Because of its decoration, a blue sky with white clouds in the Bavarian national colors, this beer tent is also called **Himmel der Bayern** (heaven for Bavarians). And yes, during two weeks it really is the Bavarian heaven :-)

In 2004 the tent was redesigned with new decorations and a new, even more beautiful sky. They also provide a balcony for smokers and the bands are „Die Kirchdorfer" and „Cagey Strings".

Beer served: Hacker-Pschorr

www.hacker-festzelt.de

6.5 Schottenhamel

 The oldest beer tent has been at the Oktoberfest since
1867. Here the traditional **Anstich** (ceremonial opening
of the first beer barrel of the festival) is performed by
Munich's mayor. You can spot many politicians (upstairs
on the balcony) and young people. This is THE tent to
go among teenagers and tweens. If you're not 20
anymore, you might feel that everyone else could be
your kid!

Waitresses wear an old-fashioned servant outfit with
white aprons and a bow in the hair. Smoking is allowed
on the balcony near the main entrance. Music is provided
by „Kapelle Otto Schwarzfischer".

Beer served: Spaten-Franziskaner

festzelt.schottenhamel.de

6.6 Winzerer Fähndl

For me this is one of the best tents, mainly because the music and vibes are great. Munich TV coverage of the Oktoberfest is done in this beer tent and with some luck, you'll appear on television.

The owners also own the beer garden at Nockherberg where you can enjoy the strong beer festival in March. The band is „Nockherberger" .

Beer served: Paulaner

www.winzerer-faehndl.com

6.7 Schützenfesthalle

A bit hidden behind the Winzerer Fähndl half-way to the Bavaria monument, this tent's seating space is only half the size of the other big beer tents because it also contains the hall where shooting clubs host their championships (Schütze means shooter).

This tent is my personal favorite. The atmosphere is always great and enthusiastic; the audience is young, but not as young as in Schottenhamel. Many members of nobility celebrate here and several charity events take place. Then virtually the whole tent is reserved for invited guests only.

Band: Die Niederalmer

Beer served: Löwenbräu

www.schuetzen-festzelt.de

6.8 Käfers Wiesn Schänke

Together with the Hippodrom this is the place where celebrities party. It's the second smallest tent with less than 3000 seats. The atmosphere is tamer than some of the other tents. Many older people, who do not dance on the ale-benches, are in the audience and rather enjoy a good conversation.

The owner of the tent also owns the delicatessen Käfer, so you'll find plenty of gourmet food you won't find in any other tent. Wine and Champagne might be match in sales volume to beer.

It is open until 1 a.m., but don't count on being let in after the other tents have closed, especially if you are already quite drunk. Of course, there's also a balcony for the smokers and celeb watching is a favorite thing to do here. Music: California Sun.

Beer served: Paulaner

www.feinkost-kaefer.de

6.9 Weinzelt - Nymphenburger Sektkellerei

As the name implies (Wein = wine, Sekt = Champagne) this is not a real beer tent. Many guests drink wine or Champagne. The music is more traditional and in general the tent is less crowded. The three bands are „Die Sumpfkröten", „Blechblos'n" and the „Högl Fun Band." In the audience are many artists and families.

This is the only tent where you don't get a **Mass** beer (1 liter), but a **Halbe** (half a liter).

Beer served: Paulaner

www.weinzelt.com

6.10 Löwenbräu

You can easily recognize the Löwenbräu tent by the huge lions on top of the tower and above the entrance. Don't be scared when the lion starts roaring!

The music is one of the most traditional ones and this tent is a favorite meeting place for the TSV 1860 soccer team. (Their nickname is "the Lions").

Music: Bert Hansmaiers Heldensteiner.

Beer served: Löwenbräu

www.loewenbraeu-festzelt.info

6.11 Pschorr – Bräurosl

For more than 100 years the Bräurosl tent is on the Wiesn and still owned by the same family.

Entertainment is big here: apart from the bands „Ludwig Thoma Musikanten" and „Südtiroler Spitzbuam", there's also an authentic Bavarian "yodeler". A guarantee for traditional Bavarian songs and lots of fun.

Beer served: Hacker-Pschorr

www.braeurosl.de

6.12 Augustinerzelt

This tent has the most traditional and authentic Bavarian folk music, therefore many native Bavarians meet here. Augustiner is supposed to be the best beer in Munich. The tent is very dark, which I don't like, but many people do.

The beer is still served from big wooden barrels, while all the other tents have long changed to steel barrels. Some say this makes it taste even better.

Music: Augustiner Oktoberfestkapelle

Beer served: Augustiner

www.augustiner-braeu.de

6.13 Ochsenbraterei

The main attraction of this tent is a whole ox being grilled (Ochse = ox, Braterei = grill). Inside, you can actually see the big turning grill. No wonder, they offer plenty of delicious ox meat dishes, even though you can get the obligatory chicken as well. This is a must to see and try.

It's also a great tent to party as much as you want with the music from „Sigertsbrunner Blasmusik" and „Die Pucher"

Beer served: Spaten

www.ochsenbraterei.de

6.14 Fischer-Vroni

Traditional food at the Oktoberfest is chicken, but here you eat fish! The famous **Steckerlfisch** is grilled in front of your eyes.

It's one of the smaller tents with great music, good food and great people. Every year on one Monday the homosexual society comes here to celebrate the Oktoberfest. Don't be surprised.

Smokers have a separate area outside with a roof. Music: Sepp Folger and musicians

Beer served: Augustiner

www.fischer-vroni.de

7 Guide to the Small Tents

Apart from the 14 big tents there are many smaller ones. The atmosphere is less rowdy, but maybe this is just what you want? Because they're less popular, it's a lot easier to find a place in one of the smaller tents.

7.1 Feisingers Kas und Weinstubn

Feisingers is a very small tent with 98 seats and 90 more in the beer garden outside. It seems more like a French tent, with cheese and wine, but definitely delicious! The raclette is the signature meal you can order here, but of course, there are also different salads, baked potatoes and schnitzel if you don't like cheese.

This is a great tent to go to for families and kids. Feisinger is proud they reserve a maximum 50 percent of the capacity, so chances are high you'll find a seat here.

7.2 Zur Bratwurst

This is a small tent with only 170 seats. As the name Bratwurst (sausage) implies, you can get all kinds of sausages, including Bavarian specialty sausages. This is not to miss if you're a first timer and want to get to know our delicious sausages. Some of them are still made over the open fire. A sight to see! And, there's a kids menu as well.

The tent looks like an old medieval house and has two floors. The „Franceso Blue Trio" pampers you with traditional music.

7.3 Glöckle Wirt

The smallest tent at Oktoberfest has only 98 seats, but it's still worth going to. Here you don't find the big party but „German Gemütlichkeit" (cosiness) like in one of those old taverns in small villages.

After 4 p.m. the „Schubiduo" plays party music.

7.4 Hendl- und Entenbraterei Heimer

As the name says, chicken and duck are the main foods on the menu. A real Bavarian duck is served with Blaukraut (red cabbage) and Knödel (dumplings). This is your chance to taste one of the best Bavarian ducks. If you're in a hurry, you can also buy the duck at the street sale.

If you want to party, this is the wrong tent for you, there's no music here, but it's a great place to sit and talk during lunch or dinner. Enjoy with your friends and have your very own party.

7.5 Poschner's Hühner und Entenbraterei

This medium-sized tent has 350 seats and an usher guides every visitor directly to a table. No searching around or standing in the alleys. This totally changes the atmosphere and makes it is more like a restaurant but with the same comfy Oktoberfest feeling as every other tent.

No music though.

7.6 Hühnerbraterei Wildmoser

Wildmoser is a Munich celebrity. The senior partner „Old Wildmoser" died in 2010, but the family still owns the Hühnerbraterei at the Wiesn. You can buy the obligatory chicken outside or you can sit in the tent with about 320 seats.

Beer is Hacker-Pschorr, and you even find a few meals for kids on the menu. The „Alpen-Casanovas" provide party music starting at 4.30 p.m..

7.7 Metzger Stubn

The Metzger Stubn (butcher's room) by the local
Vinzenz Murr butchery was added to the Wiesn in 2010.

The tent seats 130 and features all the goodies you would
normally buy at the butcher's shop, including the
Bavarian specialty *Leberkäs*. They claim to be the only
place where you can buy an authentic Leberkäs-Semmel
(meat loaf sandwich).

In the evening there's a Bavarian band with live music.

7.8 Zum Stiftl

This tent looks more like a ski hut and gives you an
après ski feeling. It has 365 seats and about 100 more
can stand at the bistro tables in the outside area.

The solo entertainer Hans Wallner takes care of fun and
entertainment in the afternoon, while after 5 p.m. a live
band plays party music.

7.9 Able's Kalbs Kuchl

The Kalbs Kuchl (veal's kitchen) offers everything made
of veal. If you want an authentic wiener schnitzel, this is
the place to go.

It is one of the newest tents, first appearing in 2008, but it already has a place in the heart of Munich locals. Great food and a place that is especially kid friendly make it a good alternative to the big tents.

In the afternoon a band plays Bavarian folk music and in the evening after 6:30 p.m. you hear the typical Wiesn songs.

The beer served is Spaten and Franziskaner Weissbier (wheat beer).

7.10 Schiebls Kaffeehaferl

With 100 seats this is one of the smallest tents, but an important one. After a long day at the Wiesn you might need a cup of coffee to freshen up. What better than to sit down here, drink a great cup of coffee and eat one of the ever-tempting German desserts?

They offer all the famous goodies like apple strudel or Dampfnudel (sweet yeast dumpling).

Between 10 a.m. and 12 a.m. you can come here for breakfast before entering one of the big beer tents.

7.11 Ammer's Hühnerbraterei

Ammer has been at Oktoberfest since 1895, which makes it the oldest chicken roastery worldwide.

Since 2000 they sell only organically grown chicken.
Apart from the classic Wiesn-Hendl you can eat all sorts
of chicken soup and other chicken delicacies.

The medium-sized tent hosts 450 guests and about the
same amount in the outside area. Starting at 6:30 p.m.
„Claudia Sommer & Band" fills the air with music and
takes care of the party feeling.

7.12 Bodos Cafézelt

This tent has a double identity. During the day they serve
breakfast starting at 9 a.m. with coffee and all kinds of
sweet delights from the traditional apple strudel to cakes
and tarts, to their own creation the (in)famous
Kirschwasser (cherry schnapps) donut. Better you don't
eat too many of them!

In the evening after 7 p.m. the tent converts into one
gigantic bar with innumerable choices of exotic
cocktails. The band „Jailhouse" takes care of the party
mood.

450 can be seated in the tent.

7.13 Wiesn Guglhupf

This tent is truly special: It's round and looks like a
gigantic bundt cake (Guglhupf), but what is more, it's a
merry-go-round! You take a seat and while eating and

drinking you're slowly turning in circles, which gives you a fantastic 360°-degree panorama of the Oktoberfest.

It is the smallest tent with only 60 seats.

7.14 Café Kaiserschmarrn

This tent looks like a sweet fairy tale castle, it is an imitation of King Ludwig II's most famous castle Neuschwanstein. It is owned by the famous Munich bakery Rischart and offers all the sweets and desserts you could ever want.

Kaiserschmarrn is a traditional Bavarian and Austrian sweet food, a cut-up and sugared pancake with raisins. One of the main attractions in this coffee-tent, is that you can watch how the Kaiserschmarrn is made in a gigantic pan.

In remembrance of the wedding of Ludwig of Bavaria and Therese of Sachsen-Hildburghausen (you remember, the royal couple who started the Oktoberfest), every day they cut a big wedding cake. It is a great experience to eat one piece and feel as if you're transported back into the past to the first Oktoberfest ever.

In the evening the coffee tent converts to a party tent with wine, Champagne and cocktails, two live bands play Oktoberfest songs and there's lots of dancing. The only thing you don't get here is beer.

7.15 Wirtshaus im Schichtl

The Schichtl is an old-fashioned magic show that has been on the Oktoberfest for ages, where during every presentation one of the visitors is „beheaded".

Besides the traditional magic show in 2006 they added a tent with beer, organically grown food and good music.

7.16 Wildstuben

Wildstuben (wild game's room) features a broad variety of game on the menu. The boar is the house specialty, and you should definitely try it.

In the evening a band plays party music. There are 200 seats and from the second floor you enjoy a great view over the Oktoberfest location.

8 What to Eat and Drink

Let me tell you one thing, there will be more than enough food and drinks to buy at Oktoberfest!

The Wiesn-Standard is a „Mass Beer" (1 liter) and half a Hendl (chicken). When you have a reservation, you have to pay in advance for a minimum consumption of two beers and half a chicken, so this is what almost everyone eats and drinks.

8.1 Drinks, Including Beer

The most obvious drink is beer, of course. The beer and the radler are served in big glass steins of one liter/one mass (approx. 1 quart) and you simply order it by saying „a Mass" (one mass). Depending on the tent, the beer price in lies between 9€ and 10€ for the liter.

But there's much more you can and should drink. In any of the tents at Oktoberfest you can get a variety of non alcoholic and alcoholic drinks.

Beer

Radler (half beer, half Sprite)

Non-Alcoholic Beer

Soft drinks (usually something called „Spezi" which is half Fanta, half Coke)

Mineral water

Schnapps

Wine and Champagne (not in all tents)

Coffee

You order all your food and drinks from the waitress, except for the schnapps. In some tents you have to get up and buy it at one of the booths along the sides of the tent or you could buy it from the "Schnapps-Girls" walking around with a vendor's tray and selling little bottles of high percentage alcohol.

At the Oktoberfest only beer from Munich breweries is sold. In fact there are six different breweries that sell beer in the tents. There are differences to the taste, so you might want to try various beers.

Below I have mentioned the six different brands and the big tents where they're sold:

Augustiner: Augustiner Tent, Fischer Vroni

Paulaner: Armbrustschützen Tent, Winzerer Fähndl, Käfer's Wiesnschänke

Spaten-Franziskaner: Hippodrom, Schottenhamel, Ochsenbraterei, Spatenbräu

Löwenbräu: Schützenfesthalle, Löwenbräu Tent

Hacker-Pschorr: Hacker Tent, Bräurosl

Hofbräu: Hofbräu Tent

Especially for the Wiesn, the breweries brew a special Oktoberfest beer. According to a friend who works in one of the tents, the recipe is secret (of course!), and every year it is adapted to the current fashion and taste of the people. For instance in the past few years Munich beer drinkers became more conscious of alcohol and calories, so the Oktoberfest beer became lighter.

Anyhow, it is still much stronger than what you're probably used to at home! Be careful!

I recommend you take a break once in a while and drink water or at least radler, this will keep your head clear for a longer time and make your visit much more enjoyable. (Well, at least if your main goal isn't to get drunk).

By the way, every big tent has an outside beer garden, where it is much easier to find a place to sit, and you can enjoy the sunshine (if there is any) and a conversation, which is not possible inside the tents.

8.2 Food

You can buy Bavarian dishes in all of the tents, ranging from 9-15 Euro. The traditional beer tent meal is half a chicken (halbes Hendl), but of course you can also have a variety of other things like dumplings, duck, pork, French fries, salads, etc.

Foods you definitely should try are:

Pretzels: The famous Bavarian pretzel (Breze) is sold in a gigantic version that is usually shared. For a table with 10 persons you would order three to four pretzels. These can be either ordered from the waitress, but there are also „Pretzels Girls" walking around with huge baskets and selling them. Either one is fine.

Obatzda: This is a special cream cheese made out of Camembert, butter, onions, and some spices. I think it tastes heavenly and is best eaten together with a pretzel.

Hendl: Typically this is half a chicken roasted on the grill. You cannot leave Oktoberfest before you have eaten this dish. It is sold everywhere.

Duck: This is half a Bavarian duck with dumplings and red cabbage.

Schweinshaxe: This dish is pork knuckle, usually served with dumplings and gravy.

Brotzeitbrettl: This is a cold meal served on a wooden tray, usually for two or more that contains different types of cheese and cold meats, radishes, gherkins and bread.

Most of the beer tents offer a "lunch special", which is a discounted menu on weekdays during lunch time. The „Mittags Wiesn menu" costs around 10 Euro. (Prices and times vary a lot in the different tents).

Throughout the part of Oktoberfest, where the fun rides are located, you find many stalls that sell different foods and snacks, as well as soft drinks, coffee and even cocktails.

8.3 Smoking

After the new German anti-smoking laws passed in 2010, smoking inside the beer tents is not allowed anymore. You can still smoke outside and in the beer gardens, but not inside.

This has been a major challenge for the owners of the beer tents. As most of the big tents have to be closed because of overfill early in the day, people cannot freely walk in and out as they wish. Once you're in you stay inside. When you leave the tent for a short smoke, you might not be allowed back in (except if you can show a valid reservation).

Many of the tents now have implemented special smokers areas either by dedicating one of the balconies to their smoking guests, or by constructing a special fenced-off area beside one of the entrances.

9 Learn the Oktoberfest Songs

What would the Oktoberfest be without the popular party songs, the Wiesnhits? They're the ones that make the crowd go crazy and dance on the benches. The popular Oktoberfest songs are repeated over and over in all of the beer tents.

People get up to stand on their beer benches and sway left and right (German: schunkeln) to the beat of the music. You'll have even more fun, if you can chant the lyrics of the songs. Most of the Oktoberfest songs are in German, but luckily for you, there are also some in English.

Every year there's a so called Wiesn Hit, supposedly the most popular song during that year's celebration. If you learn the lyrics (at least the chorus) of a few popular Oktoberfest songs, you will have a lot more fun celebrating. By the way, the melody isn't as important, with thousands of persons trying to sing as loud as possible, nobody will notice, if you are off-key.

Below you find some of the classic Oktoberfest hits, the ones that have moved millions of people over the years and are repeated every year. If you learn the lyrics once, you can sing those songs basically forever.

9.1 Skandal im Sperrbezirk by the Spider Murphy Gang

This is easily the most popular Oktoberfest song ever. Skandal im Sperrbezirk (Scandal in the Off-Limits Area) by the Spider Murphy Gang, a Munich rock band, was a German Number One hit in the early eighties and is still alive and kicking every year on the Wiesn.

By the way, the phone number mentioned in the song text had to be blocked in Munich, because thousands of people tried to call it.

This Oktoberfest song has so much power, that it was forbidden in the tents for a few years, due to security reasons. Imagine thousands of people frenetically hopping up and down on the wooden beer benches, and you get the idea.

Lyrics to Skandal im Sperrbezirk

In München steht ein Hofbräuhaus,
doch Freudenhäuser müssen raus,
damit in dieser schönen Stadt
das Laster keine Chance hat.
Doch jeder ist gut informiert,
weil Rosi täglich inseriert,
und wenn dich deine Frau nicht liebt:
Wie gut das es die Rosi gibt!
Und draußen vor der großen Stadt
steh'n die Nutten sich die Füsse platt.
Skandal im Sperrbezirk!
Skandal im Sperrbezirk!
Skandal – Skandal um Rosi.

Ja, Rosi hat ein Telefon,
auch ich hab ihre Nummer schon,
unter 32-16-8
herrscht Konjunktur die ganze Nacht.
Und draußen im Hotel d'Amour
langweilen sich die Damen nur,
weil jeder, den die Sehnsucht quält
ganz einfach Rosis Nummer wählt.
Und draußen vor der großen Stadt
steh'n die Nutten sich die Füße platt
Skandal im Sperrbezirk!
Skandal im Sperrbezirk!
Skandal – Skandal um Rosi.

9.2 Ein Prosit der Gemütlichkeit

This song is the one liked best by the beer tent owners
and breweries. Apparently someone has calculated that
each time it is played, 1000 liters of beer are swallowed.

I'm not sure if these numbers are correct, but whenever
the band plays "Ein Prosit" (and they do it often) you
are supposed to stand up, toast with everyone and take a
big mouthful from your stein.

Lyrics to Ein Prosit der Gemütlichkeit

Ein Prosit, ein Prosit
Der Gemütlichkeit
Ein Prosit, ein Prosit
Der Gemütlichkeit.
Oans, zwoa, drei, Gsuffa!

9.3 Marmor, Stein und Eisen Bricht
by Drafi Deutscher

This is a really old song! It was first recorded in 1965, and I believe it has been an Oktoberfest song ever since. Because the song has been there for such a long time, virtually every German visitor knows it. You'll rarely find anyone who doesn't.

Lyrics to Marmor, Stein und Eisen Bricht

Weine nicht, wenn der Regen fällt
(Dam Dam, Dam Dam)
Es gibt einen der zu Dir hält
(Dam Dam, Dam Dam)

Marmor, Stein und Eisen bricht
aber unsere Liebe nicht
alles, alles geht vorbei
doch wir sind uns treu

Kann ich einmal nicht bei dir sein
(Dam Dam, Dam Dam)
Denk daran, du bist nicht allein
(Dam Dam, Dam Dam)

Marmor, Stein und Eisen bricht
aber unsere Liebe nicht

alles, alles geht vorbei
doch wir sind uns treu

Nimm den goldenen Ring von mir
(Dam Dam, Dam Dam)
Er war teuer dass sag ich dir
(Dam Dam, Dam Dam)

Marmor, Stein und Eisen bricht
aber unsere Liebe nicht
alles, alles geht vorbei
doch wir sind uns treu

10 How to Make a Reservation

Sadly, the Oktoberfest has become the victim of its own popularity: especially on weekends, the beer tents fill up quickly and are closed early. The surest way to get in is to have a reservation. You need to make your reservations months in advance, otherwise you will be much too late. Nevertheless, you can check the official Munich site for information; maybe you'll get lucky.

If you want to make a reservation, you first have to pick the beer tent you'd like to visit. Usually, you need to write a letter or fax to the tent administrators because they won't accept reservations either by phone or online.

To find out the exact procedure, check the websites for contact addresses and/or instructions. For you convenience I have provided links to the websites of all 14 big beer tents.

The fax needs to include **number of people**, as well as **date** and **time** you'd like to reserve.

Number of persons: The minimum number for Oktoberfest reservations is 10 (one table) and can be done only in multiples of 10.

Date: You can chose one or more dates; it's much more probable to get a reservation on weekdays than on weekends

Time: There are two blocks of time that can be reserved; noon till 4 p.m. or 4 p.m. until end. The times slightly vary from tent to tent. And of course, it is much easier to get a reservation in the afternoon than in the evening.

A few weeks to months later, you'll receive an answer from them, either with your confirmation or with a polite letter telling you that, unfortunately, they couldn't give you a reservation, and sometimes they'll offer an alternative.

For example they could say: "Unfortunately we were not able to allocate you on Friday night, but we still have empty tables on Thursday afternoon."

10.1 When to Make an Oktoberfest Reservation?

Usually, the beer tents gather all requests during **January** and **February**; and allocate the tables in March.

But you might still be able to reserve a table during weekdays in the afternoon, even in June or July. Some tents have a waiting list and will call/write you if someone has canceled a reservation. Even though this sounds unbelievable, it happens. Normally, there are companies that habitually reserve tables each year and for some reason or another need to cancel all or at least some of their seats.

10.2 How Much Does an Oktoberfest Reservation Cost?

You actually don't pay for the reservation, but for the consumption. With each seat you have to buy a minimum of two beers and half a chicken, which costs about 30€ (40 USD) per person.

Those prepaid beer and food vouchers are sent to you once you confirm and pay for your reservation. The vouchers are valid during the whole Oktoberfest period and even afterwards in specific restaurants in Munich that are owned by the issuing beer tent company.

But I'm sure you won't have any left. :-)

Of course, your can make reservations for 10 and only go in a group of seven. Usually, the waitress will request you to allow to to three other people to sit at your table when she sees your group doesn't add up to 10.

11 How to Get Inside Without a Reservation

Don't despair! It's still very possible to get into the tents even without a reservation if you just follow a few rules.

The city of Munich requires beer tent owners to keep one third of the seats in the central aisle unreserved during weekdays and all of them on weekends.

11.1 Tips and Tricks

With a small group you can get into any beer tent and find a space at the table with other people if you follow these rules:

Go on weekdays: Weekends and especially Saturdays, the beer tents are packed and close early.

Go early: If you arrive before 2 p.m., you should always find a table to sit down.

Try the side entrances: Don't stand in line for hours at the main entrance; instead check out if they're letting in people somewhere else.

Be friendly and smile: Bouncers tend to let in people they like, and if you're already drunk, your chances of getting inside any tent are next to zero.

Never try to get in with a big group: I would say five to six people maximum. If you're a bigger group, split up and meet again later inside.

Try various tents: If your favorite beer tent is already closed, go to another one. They're all great.

Once you're inside the tent, you've already passed the biggest challenge. Now you can freely walk around and search for a place to sit down. But there's a big but: You cannot just stand around because beer is sold only at the tables.

Look for a table in the part that says "without reservation." These tables are usually in the middle of the tents near the band. The advantage is that you can stay there as long as you want. If the unreserved tables are already taken, you can sit at any of the tables along the sides the Oktoberfest beer tents twhere reservations start at at 4 p.m. Here, you have to leave about a half hour before the reservations begin.

When the tent is already full, but you somehow managed to sneak in, then you'll have to share a table with another party.

Ask nicely whether the people will allow you to sit at their table. Don't get discouraged; you might have to ask at five to 10 different tables.

Ask the waitress whether she has a place for you somewhere (if you find one who seems to be in a good mood).

OK, but you arrived in Munich on a Saturday after 5 p.m. and just have to go to Oktoberfest. Well, if nothing else works out, you can still sit outside the beer gardens of the big tents or try one of the smaller tents.

By the way, Viator just recently started offering tours to the Munich Oktoberfest with reserved tables. Read my review of the Viator Oktoberfest Toursat www.inside-munich.com/of-tours and check out if they still have tickets available.

If you're still unhappy and desperately want an Oktoberfest reservation, there are some companies like Worldticketshop that sell tickets on the so-called second market. The prices are usually quite hefty, but you decide, if it's worth it.

12 What to Wear

You can wear whatever you wish at the Oktoberfest. Many wear jeans and sneakers.

Of course, we Bavarians like to dress up with traditional dirndl and lederhose, but it's in no way a must to do so.

Many foreign visitors wear dirndl and lederhose, the traditional Bavarian clothing. Some of the strictest and most conservative Bavarians oppose this and think only the real Bavarians should wear Tracht (costumes).

But almost everyone else is just happy and thinks it's fabulous that our visitors go with the spirit of the Oktoberfest and try to fit in as much as possible by wearing traditional clothing. By the way, most of the Tracht you can buy nowadays are not the authentic traditional Bavarian clothing, but a modern adaptation of it.

See what one of my readers wrote:

Oktoberfest 2009
by: der Herman
"We went to the Wiesn, wearing Tracht and had a great time. I speak some German, and the people seemed warm to the fact that I was wearing Lederhosen and my wife, Kel, was wearing a (self made) Dirndl. I even got the impression that they preferred us to the 'Preußen'. One local taught me some Bavarian songs, and was surprised that I already knew and sung well some Oktoberfest songs (I learned them before we left). We had a GREAT time and want to go again and spend more time there! "

12.1 Dirndl Dress

Dirndl is the Bavarian word for girl and because formerly all women wore this dress, it was given the same name. The traditional style consists of a wide and long skirt with a corsage, a white blouse and a colorful apron. Today you can buy dirndls in all styles, materials, lengths and prices. It can cost anywhere from 100 euros (including blouse and apron) up to several thousand euros.

Originally the dirndl was the **working dress** of female servants. Even today it's the uniform for waitresses not only during Oktoberfest, but also in many traditional Bavarian restaurants and beer halls. Therefore, the fabric usually is a very strong cotton.

Up until a few years ago, the blouse was always white, but then red and black transparent blouses became fashionable. Personally, I prefer the white ones. The apron is slightly shorter than the skirt and is tied with a large knot (Schleife).

Blouse and apron knots have one additional important function, they let everyone know the wearer's availability. We really make it easy for the flirtatious, right?

Knot on the left and/or upper blouse button open means the girl's single and open to flirting.

Knot on the right and/or all blouse buttons closed means she's in a relationship, and you'd better not try.

Knot on the back means you're dealing with a widow (or a waitress).

Knot on the front is reserved for a virgin.

12.2 Lederhosen (leather trousers)

Lederhosen are the traditional male trousers in Bavaria. Lately, you can see many women wearing them too. Leather trousers are usually shorts or knickerbockers; very rarely do you see them in a long style. The traditional ones are usually braided or embroidered with Bavarian motifs like the edelweiss (a flower from the Alps) and have suspenders.

Due to the quality of the leather (and the high price!) the typical Bavarian man buys only one lederhose in his adult life. It will last forever, and is usually never washed. My friends keep telling my that a lederhose gets better when it soaks up beer and dirt.

The male attire is completed by a shirt, socks and shoes. The shirts are either white or have the typical red or blue checkered patterns. Socks go up to the knee and look hand-knitted. The authentic shoes to wear are Haferlschuhe, but you can also wear any kind of normal shoes; just leave the sneakers at home, because you will look like a tourist. :-)

13 Oktoberfest with Kids

Unlike what you might have seen or heard in the media, the Oktoberfest is a great place for kids.

A small part of Theresienwiese near the southeast entrance is reserved for families and kids. At the "family corner" you find food and drinks for little ones as well as carousels, miniscooters and places for changing diapers.

Kids are allowed in the beer tents as long as they're accompanied by their parents. Many tents offer kids' meals during lunch time and have special treats for them. Last year, our son received a little golden crown in one of the tents. He was soooo proud!

A beer tent in the evening, when the party is going on and people dance on the tables (many of them drunk), is not a place for kids though. You wouldn't bring them to a night club or dance bar either, would you?

Keep in mind that strollers and prams are allowed only until 6 p.m. and not at all on Saturday or when the Oktoberfest ground are very crowded.

14 Where to Stay

14.1 Hotels and Hostels

During Oktoberfest it's next to impossible to find a hotel room if you haven't reserved a few months in advance. Apart from being scarce, prices shoot sky high, and you'll have to pay double or triple the normal room rates. Spontaneous visitors might have to stay as far away as Augsburg or Ingolstadt, and even there, accommodation prices are astronomical.

The one tip I can give you is to book your hotel early!

Even the hostels become quite pricey, and you can end up paying 100 USD for a bed in a eight-bed dorm room! Check at www.inside-munich.com/of-hostels if there are still available rooms.

14.2 Campgrounds and Mobile Homes

If you love nature and prefer independence, you can stay at several camping grounds around the city in beautiful locations like the Isarauen in Thalkirchen (near the zoo) or Langwieder See. All of them are easily reachable via public transport.

If you want to camp with your own tent, you can try the campground in Thalkirchen that's very nice and quiet during the night (no big party!)

The campground in Obermenzing hosts the Stoke Campgrounds. They offer already setup two-person tents with sleeping mats and bags, including breakfast, barbecue and shuttle bus to Oktoberfest grounds for 50€ per night.

It seems that the main focus of the whole Stoke is getting drunk (judging from the website). After the beer tents close, you can continue the party with flat fee drinking on their grounds. If this is what you want, fine. Personally, I wouldn't. Oktoberfest is much more than drinking, and you can have lots of fun without getting completely drunk.

When arriving with your own mobile home, don't even think of parking in the city center as virtually all areas inside the Mittlerer Ring are now restricted parking for anyone except residents of that area. Furthermore, you're not allowed to sleep in your camper anyway anywhere in Munich. You will face hefty fines and might even get towed away.

Apart from the campgrounds there is a big area in the southeast of Munich where you can stay with your camper: the Oktoberfest Campground in München Riem, De-Gasperi-Bogen offers space for 1500 campers, about half of them with a power connection. They have sanitary facilities, a supermarket and a few restaurants. The price is 35 euros per camper, including two people and 15 euros per additional person. Reservations are possible but not necessary.

Website: www.oktoberfest-camping.com

14.3 Private Rooms

The company Wimdu offers private rooms. Now you can travel like a local and stay in fully equipped apartments, that are cheaper than hotel rooms of a similar quality. You might even get some insider tips from your host. Wimdu is a reputable company that checks out the apartments and owners before allowing them into their catalog.

15 Party after Midnight

Oktoberfest tents close at 11 p.m., and many people just go home. If you enter the tents at 11 a.m., then you can celebrate 12 hours and drink a lot of beer. For most, this is enough.

But, if you want to go on partying, then there are many options in Munich such as the famous night club P1, which offers an After Wiesn party every night. Anyone dressed in a dirndl and lederhosen has free entry.

Das Wiesnzelt in the Löwenbräu brewery at Stiglmaierplatz. claims to have the original Oktoberfest feeling with a live band, all the Oktoberfest songs and great beer. Tickets can be booked in advance and are 38€, including 16€ food voucher.

16 First Timer? Follow These Tips.

If you're planning to visit the Oktoberfest for the first time, there are a few things you should keep in mind. Following these tips will help you to have a pleasant stay at Munich's famous beer festival.

Carry Your ID

I never had my ID card checked when entering Oktoberfest tents, but this doesn't mean it can't happen. It will happen if you end up in some kind of emergency. When you want to continue celebrating in one of the night clubs, they regularly check it (especially if you look young).

Always take a friend or more with you

Even though most of the people are friendly and peaceful, there's the occasional drunk who can cause trouble. Being with a friend makes your stay much safer (a woman especially should never go alone). Furthermore, it's a lot more fun to celebrate with your friends than with strangers.

Drink a lot of water

The old rule "one beer, one water" also applies for the biggest beer festival in the world. The beer tents are hot and you'll be thirsty. Drinking only beer makes you drunk much faster than you even notice, especially when you're not used to the strong German beer.

Be friendly to the waitress

Waitresses in the beer tents are the secret queens of the Oktoberfest. They decide whether you can stay or have to leave. And they definitely decide if you get a beer or not. Remember that you can only order beer once you sit at a table. No beer is sold to anyone standing in the alleys.

Do everything that requires coordination before the second beer

It's not funny to be trapped inside a roller coaster after the second or third beer. Owners of the attractions will not let you inside anyways, because they know what can happen.

Enjoy!

Dance and sing as much as you want and have a lot of fun.

Don't bring valuables

Bring only the amount of money you're planning to spend. Don't wear expensive jewelry. Wherever there are masses of people, there are also pickpockets. Be on the look out.

Don't drink and drive

Use the public transport for your sake and the sake of everyone else who could be involved in an accident with you. Drunk driving will cause you to lose your drivers license and get you into a lot of trouble. Germans are very tolerant about alcohol but not in connection with driving.

17 About the Author

Marion Kummerow has moved to Munich more than 15 years ago, where she met her future husband during a visit to the Oktoberfest. Since then she has lived in different parts of Munich with her family.

In 2004 she and her husband started the website www.inside-munich.com, in order to show the beauties of Munich to foreign visitors.

She has put all of her knowledge about Munich and the Oktoberfest into this guide book, to help her readers have the time of their live at Oktoberfest.

" We visit the Oktoberfest every year since more than 15 years and we still find something new every time", says Marion Kummerow., "now you can profit from our experience."

Thank you for purchasing my book. Please review this book on Amazon.

I use your feedback to make the next version better. Thank you so much!

Become a Fan on Facebook

http://www.facebook.com/InsideMunichGuide and never miss an important update.

„To get more tips about Munich and the Oktoberfest, click the link below to subscribe to our newsletter."

http://inside-munich.com/tips

Also by Marion Kummerow

German Christmas Traditions

A comprehensive book on German Christmas traditions with very personal views from the author who was born and raised in Germany. Here you find everthing you always wanted to know about German Christmas, including four of the best Christmas Cookie recipes and the lyrics to three famous German Christmas Carols.

How to Rent An Apartement in Munich

The detailed step-by-step instructions in How to Rent an Apartment in Munich: Multiply Your Chances to Move into Your Dream Apartment map out your move to Germany for you. The helpful glossary of German words will help you communicate with lessors.